250 Quizzes For Couples: How Well Do You Really Know Me?
Created by Natalie Styles

All rights reserved.
No part of this publication may be reproduced, stored in a retrievalsystem or transmitted in any form or by any means, electronic,mechanical, photocopying, recording or otherwise, withoutprior permission of the author.

Insights contained in this book shouldn't be taken as proffesional advice.

ISBN: 979-8594882232

First Edition
January 2021

May this book bring you joy, fun & laugh.

Natalie

Contents

Introduction..4

How To Use This Book?..5

Chapter 1 - Easy Questions About Everyday Life.......................6

Chapter 2 - Throwback To When We Met................................11

Chapter 3 - Food Checkup..15

Chapter 4 - This Or That..19

Chapter 5 - Who Is Most Likely To..24

Chapter 6 - Future And Past...28

Chapter 7 - What Happens In Bed, Stays In Bed.....................31

Chapter 8 - My Favorite F Words Are Family And Friends...35

Chapter 9 - Would Your Partner Rather?.................................39

Chapter 10 - True Or False..44

Partner 1 Answers...48

Partner 2 Answers...60

About The Author..72

Introduction

250 Quizzes For Couples: How Well Do You Really Know me? *i*s a book that has been designed for every couple that would like to know each other better. In this book you will find lots of questions related to your partner. It's a perfect conversation starter for each couple who loves to talk about big and small things of their life. Communication in relationship is really important - that's why this book comes in handy for everyone.

How many times your better half asked you a question about themselves and you didn't know the answer? Once? Twice? Or maybe more? It is always something new to learn about your partner. And that's absolutely understandable that sometimes we don't know things that we should. That's why I've created this book. You will find there many questions - easy and really hard ones. By completing this book together you will discover new things and strengthen your relationship.

Remember to not compete with each other - that's not the point of this book. You can sum up your scores, but don't take it too seriously - results are only to show you the topics you should take a longer conversation about. Listen to each other and talk not only about the questions, but also about things that come up to your minds while taking a quiz.

How To Use This Book?

You will find 250 questions and 10 chapters inside. In the beginning page of each chapter, you will see a short instruction how to do the quiz and answer the questions. There are various types of questions in this book. Most of them are short-answer quizzes, but you will also find multiple choice questions, true or false, would you rather and more.

There are two ways you can answer the questions:

Option 1.
In the end of this book, there are special sheets, where you can easily note down your answers. There is a section for Partner 1 and Partner 2, so you have to decide who is who.

Option 2.
If you don't want to write in the book, you can both take an empty sheet of paper and note down the answers.

After each quiz is completed and your answers are noted down, you can check them with each other and see who has got a better score. Take a conversation about each question and discuss questions that were difficult for you. Remember that this is a book that should give you fun and laugh while answering, so don't feel pressured. Now decide who is Partner 1 and who is Partner 2 and start the game!

Chapter 1

Easy Questions About Everyday Life

There are many topics for us, that are really easy to answer. Starting from the date of birth and finishing on favorite store at mall. These things should be obvious for our other half, but are they really are?

In this chapter you will find a quiz about your partner's life, habits, favorite things to do and more. This quiz should be the easiest of all of them. There are only short-answers questions and a few multiple choice ones.

Answer the questions, check the answers with your partner and sum up the points. Remember that all your answers should be about your partner and vice versa. Do not answer the questions as if they were about you. When you are finished, read your answer and your partner will confirm it when it's correctly.

1. What is your parnter's middle name?

2. What does your partner like better?
a) Tea   b) Coffee

3. What is your partner's favorite color?

4. What is the color of your partner's eyes?

5. Name your partner's favorite movie actor/actress.

6. What is your partner's favorite season?
a) Fall   b) Spring   c) Summer   d) Winter

7. Where does your partner fell better?
a) In the city   b) In the countryside

8. Name a food your partner could eat everyday.

Easy Questions About Everyday Life

9. What is your partner's favorite animal?
a) Cat   b) Dog   c) Horse   d) Other

10. Your partner is a:
a) morning person   b) night owl

11. Where does your partner prefer to spend vacation?
a) by the sea   b) in the mountains
c) on the lake   d) in the village

12. What is your partner's favorite type of sport?

13. In your partner's free time, they like to:
a) relax   b) be active

14. What does your partner prefer? Reading books or watching movies?

15. What is your partner's favorite movie?

16. Name a netflix series your partner could watch every single day.

17. Your partner prefers when it's:
a) cold   b) hot

18. What is your partner favorite day of the week?

19. How many children your partner would like to have?

20. What is your partner's shoe size?

21. How tall is your partner?

22. Your partner is:
a) right-handed   b) left-handed

23. What is your partner's best friend's name?

24. What languages does your partner speak?

25. What's your partner's favorite song?

26. How many partners before you, have your partner had?

27. Your partner prefers to:
a) send a text message   b) call

28. What is your partner's biggest dream?

29. What is your partner's addiction?

30. Your partner is an:
a) introvert   b) extrovert

Chapter 2

Throwback To When We Met

First meeting, first date, first kiss... These are really important moments in our lives! We all had butterflies in our stomach and were trying to be as best as we could. Some people remember all of the first times and things in common with their partner, while some people don't. How about you?

In this chapter you will find a quiz about you both and your relationship. There are only short-answer questions, so you have to really think about the answers. No worries if you don't remember something! It is a great time to go back to the beginning of **YOU**, and talk about it.

Answer the questions, check the answers with your partner - whether your answers are the same, and sum up the points. If your answers are different, then take a conversation about it and decide who was right.

31. What is the date we met each other?

32. Where and when was our first date?

33. Do you remember what was your partner's first thought about you when they saw you for the first time?

34. What is the thing we never done alone before, but tried for the first time together?

35. Where did we go for our first vacation?

36. What was our the most romantic moment?

37. When did we kiss for the first time?

38. After how long after starting dating, did we have sex?

39. Where was that?

40. When did your partner feel for the first time that this is "it"?

41. What did you receive from your partner for your last birthday?

42. What do we like to do the most in our free time?

43. What do you like, but I actually hate?

44. How did we spent our first Valentine's Day?

45. When did your partner meet your parents?

46. Who said "I love you" first?

47. Who is more sensitive?

48. What is our biggest dream?

49. Countries we've been together.

50. When would we like to get married?

51. Where should it be?

52. How do you like to call your partner when you are alone?

52. What is a thing we would like to try to do in the future?

53. Who is a better cook?

54. What in your opinion, did your relationship taught your partner?

Chapter 3

Food Checkup

Who doesn't like food? I mean, eating is a part of everyone's life. When we are in a relationship, we usually know why our partner doesn't like tomatoes and why Chinese food is the best in their opinion.

In this chapter you will find a quiz about food, drinks and eating. So don't wait any longer and order pizza right now! There are multiple choice questions and short-answer as well. If you spend a lot of time with each other, you should easily answer everything.

Answer the questions, check the answers with your partner and sum up the points. Remember that all your answers should be about your partner and vice versa. Do not answer the questions as if they were about you. When you are finished, read your answer and your partner will confirm it when it's correctly . Who loses, pays for next dinner!

55. If your partner had to eat something, they would like it to be:
a) spicy   b) sweet   c) sour   d) mild

56. What is your partner's most liked dinner?

57. What would your partner never eat?

58. What is your partner's favorite alcoholic drink?
a) gin   b) beer   c) vodka   d) vine

59. Your partner is always down for:
a) pizza   b) burgers   c) Chinese food

60. What is your partner's favorite breakfast?

61. Your partner prefers:
a) vegetables   b) fruits

Food Checkup

62. Your partner's would choose:
a) sweets   b) snacks

63. What is your partner's favorite ice cream favor?

64. The best food your partner ever eaten.

65. Where was that?

66. What is your partner's favorite restaurant?

67. Your partner prefers:
a) soda   b) water   c) juice

68. Your partner's less favorite vegetable.

69. What kitchen your partner likes the most?

70. What can your partner cook best?

Food Checkup

71. Does your partner like sea food?

72. What food is your partner allergic to?

73. Who eats more, me or you?

74. Who would eat the last slice of pizza?

75. Your partner would prefer to go to:
a) bar   b) restaurant   c) fast food   d) cafe

76. What is your partner's favorite fast food?

77. The worst food your partner ever eaten.

78. Your partner is always down for:
a) chocolate cake b) cookies c) ice creams

79. Your partner prefers:
a) sparkling water   b) still water

Chapter 4

This or That

Cats or dogs? Day or night? Spanish or Germany? I think there is nothing to explain about these questions.

In this chapter you will find a quiz about absolutely everything. There are only questions that require quick shots from you. Don't think too much, and say whatever comes to your head first.

Answer the questions, check the answers with your partner and sum up the points. Remember that all your answers should be about your partner and vice versa. For instance, in a question *"Soda or Water?" you note down what you think your partner prefers, not what you do prefer.* Do not answer the questions as if they were about you. When you are finished, read your answer and your partner will confirm it when it's correctly.

80. Cats or dogs?

81. Rock music or pop music?

82. Hot chocolate or tea?

83. Day or night?

84. Winter or summer?

85. Book or movie?

86. Theatre or cinema?

87. Car or motorcycle?

88. Horror or comedy?

89. Singing or dancing?

90. PC or tablet?

91. Gold or silver?

92. 70's or 80's?

93. Burgers or pizza?

94. Toasts or waffles?

95. Skiing or snowboarding?

96. Sweet or salty?

97. Take a shower or take a bath?

98. Cardio or weights?

99. Cake or cookies?

100. Party or movie night?

101. Laundry or dishes?

102. Online shopping or in store shopping?

103. Email or letter?

104. Toilet paper: over or under?

105. Milk or hot chocolate?

106. Plane or train?

107. Ocean or sea?

108. City or countryside?

109. Delivery or dine in?

110. Book or ebook?

111. Bicycle or roller skates?

112. Sun or snow?

113. Black or white?

114. Zoo or water park?

115. Apartment or house?

116. Credit card or cash?

117. Christmas or Halloween?

118. Serious or funny?

119. Money or happiness?

Chapter 5

Who Is Most Likely To

There are situations and things in every couple's life, that one of the partners is always most likely to do something. Personally, I would never ever in my life touch a spider, but my partner definitely would do.

In this chapter you will find some questions about various habits, situations and other things. In each question, you have to answer who is most likely to do something. That's an easy one!

Answer the questions, check the answers with your partner - whether your answers are the same, and sum up the points. If your answers are different, then take a conversation about it and decide who was right.

120. Who is most likely to get drunk?

121. Who is most likely to become rich?

122. Who is most likely to be a drama queen?

123. Who is most likely to have more tattoos?

124. Who is most likely to do weird things in public?

125. Who is most likely to fail an easy test?

126. Who is most likely to cry after a sad movie?

127. Who is most likely to cook a romantic dinner?

128. Who is most likely to forget an anniversary?

129. Who is most likely to write a love poem?

130. Who is most likely to yell during an argument?

131. Who is most likely to lose weight?

132. Who is most likely to buy useless things?

133. Who is most likely to drop their phone in a toilet?

134. Who is most likely to wear pajamas all day?

135. Who is most likely to snore?

136. Who is most likely to forget people's names?

137. Who is most likely to eat a bug?

138. Who is most likely to forget about brushing their teeth in the morning?

139. Who is most likely to become a vegetarian?

140. Who is most likely to fake an orgasm?

141. Who is most likely to end up alone?

142. Who is most likely to sing in the shower?

Who Is Most Likely To

Chapter 6

Future and Past

Conversations about past and future are very often difficult. Sometimes we don't remember something, sometimes we don't want to talk about something, and sometimes we do don't know what we would like to happen in the future. Try to remind yourselves important moments of your lives that have happened in the past before you start the quiz.

In this chapter you will find a really short quiz about things that already happened, and things that are going to happen. There are only short-answer questions about moments of your lives that you should have talked about before.

Answer the questions, check the answers with your partner and sum up the points. Remember that most of your answers should be about your partner and vice versa. Do not answer the questions as if they were about you. When you are finished, read your answer and your partner will confirm it when it's correctly.

143. Who was a shy child?

144. What is the name of your partner's first love?

145. Where was your partner born?

146. What was your partner's first real job?

147. What was your partner's hobby when they were a child?

148. Name a thing your partner couldn't live without in the future.

149. Who was your partner's first celebrity crush?

150. Who doesn't want to live in their native country in the future?

151. What is your partner's best memory from childhood?

152. What is the coolest country your partner has visited?

153. What places would your partner visit in the future?

154. When does your partner would like to take next step related to you in the future?

155. What was your partner's favorite subject at school?

156. Did your partner have any pets in their childhood home?

157. Who wants to have more kids in the future?

Chapter 7

What Happens In Bed, Stays In Bed

Intimacy is truly important in every relationship. Very often it's a taboo subject for a lot of us. Unnecessarily. Sex is something we should talk about and discuss our fantasies and problems. I mean, is anybody who should know our bodies better than our partner? Take this quiz seriously and don't be afraid to talk about your sex life.

In this chapter you will find a quiz about intimacy. You will find short-answer questions and multiple choice ones. Be honest while answering.

Answer the questions, check the answers with your partner and sum up the points. Remember that all your answers should be about your partner and vice versa. When you are finished, read your answer and your partner will confirm it when it's correctly. After this quiz, a good option would be to take a long break in your bedroom...

158. Who loves to have sex more often?

159. Who is most likely to initiate sex?

160. Your partner's favorite sex position is:
a) doggie-style   b) missionary
c) cowgirl   d) other

161. Who is most likely to have sex in changing room?

162. What's your partner's biggest fantasy about you?

163. What's something non-sexual, that turns your partner on?

164. Your partner would prefer to have:
a) sex in bed   b) sex in a random place

165. Is there any erotic movie that turns your partner on?

166. What's your partner's perfect time to have sex?
a) in the morning   b) in the afternoon
c) at night

167. How many people your partner slept with?

168. Name a thing your partner would never try at bed.

169. Does your partner like/would like to try anal sex?

170. Does your partner like when you are rough?

33   What Happens In Bed, Stays In Bed

171. What best describes your partner?
a) submissive   b) taking control

172. If your partner had an opportunity to have sex with you here and now, he would prefer:
a) quickie   b) marathon session

173. Who is most likely to send nudes?

174. Your partner would prefer to watch:
a) 50 Shades of Grey   b) 50 Shades of Black

175. Your partner prefers:
a) dirty messages   b) naked pictures

176. How old was your partner when they lost their virginity?

177. What's your partner less favorite position?

Chapter 8

My Favorite F Words Are Family And Friends

Is anything more important than family and friends? Being among your loved ones brings us joy, laugh and fun. I cannot imagine my life without people I really adore in my life. How about you? Do you really know who is your partner's best friend and what's your partner's mom middle name?

In this chapter you will find a quiz about relations with family members and friends. There are mostly short-answer questions and a few multiple choice ones. This chapter may remind you of some emotional moments, that's why you have to remember, that you are taking this quiz with your loved one that will always support you.

Answer the questions, check the answers with your partner and sum up the points. Remember that all your answers should be about your partner and vice versa. When you are finished, read your answer and your partner will confirm it when it's correctly.

178. What's more important for your partner?
a) friends   b) family

179. What are the middle names of your partner's parents?

180. How many siblings does your partner have?

181. What is the perfect time for your partner to get married?

182. When would your partner like to have kids?

183. Did your partner get pocket money in childhood?

184. What's your partner's best memory with their family?

185. Who is the funniest person in your partner's family?

186. Your partner has:
a) a lot of colleagues   b) a few friends

187. What's the name of your partner's closest friend?

188. How does your partner spend time with their friends?

189. Name a person your partner likes the most of your friends.

190. Does your partner like your friends?

191. What's your partner best memory related to their friends?

192. Were your partner's parents strict in their childhood?

193. What's your partner's best friend from childhood?

194. Your partner has more:
a) female friends   b) male friends

195. Where did your partner and their parents go for the first vacation?

196. Has your partner ever met their great grandparents?

197. Is your partner shy when among your friends?

198. Has your partner ever had a dog?

Chapter 9

Would Your Partner Rather?

Would you rather questions are always fun. Why? Because there are no wrong answers! How about would your partner rather questions? Do you really believe you know what would your partner choose?

In this chapter you will find questions about totally weird things. You will always have an option between two statements, and your only task is to choose one of them that suits your partner best.

Answer the questions, check the answers with your partner and sum up the points. Remember that all your answers should be about your partner and vice versa. When you are finished, read your answer and your partner will confirm it when it's correctly.

199. Would your partner rather live in a desert island or in a tree house in the jungle?

200. Would your partner rather never be able to eat fruits or never be able to eat vegetables anymore?

201. Would your partner rather eat an old egg or eat extremely spicy jalapeno?

202. Would your partner rather eat a jar of peanut butter or a jar of honey?

203. Would your partner rather lose their best friend or lose their partner?

204. Would your partner rather to be always too hot or too cold outside?

205. Would your partner rather be unable to have kids or only be able to have twins?

206. Would your partner rather never use social media again or never watch TV again?

207. Would your partner rather stay in or go out for a date?

208. Would you partner rather to have a daughter or a son?

209. Would your partner rather be constantly hungry and never be able to eat or constantly sleepy and never be able to sleep?

210. Would your partner rather live without dishwasher or live without a washing machine?

211. Would your partner rather live without the internet or live without television?

212. Would your partner rather give up watching Netflix for a year or give up playing video games for a year?

213. Would your partner rather be forever alone for the rest of your life or always be surrounded by fake friends?

214. Would your partner rather have unlimited pizza for life or unlimited tacos for life?

215. Would your partner rather forget your birthday or you forget your partner's birthday?

216. Would your partner rather be a vegan for a week or eat only meat for a week?

217. Would your partner be rich or happy?

218. Would your partner rather never celebrate Christmas again or never celebrate Halloween again?

219. Would your partner rather listen to the same song to the rest of their life or don't listen to music again at all?

220. Would your partner rather have a wedding at the beach or in the beautiful palace?

221. Would your partner rather marry their ex or be forever alone?

222. Would your partner rather get matching tattoos or matching piercing?

Chapter 10
True Or False

Do you know this feeling when you read something on Instagram and you already know that this statement suits your partner, so you send him a screen shot of this? Or when you make sausages for breakfast and you know, without even asking him about it, that your partner will eat two of them with ton of ketchup? That's what this quiz will be about - things that come to our mind.

This is the last chapter of this book and you will find here lot's of true or false statements. Each statement is assigned to one of the partners, and your task is to go through all of them, and say whether they are true or false.

Answer the questions, check the answers with your partner and sum up the points. Remember that you have to answer all of the questions - also the ones that are about you. If you haven't decided who is Partner 1 and who is Partner 2 yet, do it now and have fun!

After finishing this quiz, sum up all of the scores of all the quizzes, and check who is the winner of **250 Quizzes For Couples: How Well Do You Really Know Me?**

TRUE **FALSE**

223. Partner 1 is a greater muddler.

224. Partner 2 has more friends.

225. Partner 1 is less lazy.

226. Partner 2 is very energetic.

227. Partner 1 has more ex partners.

228. Partner 2 has never eaten sea food.

229. Partner 1 loves to travel.

230. Partner 2 has never been to Australia.

231. Partner 1 gets drunk after 2 drinks.

232. Partner 2 complains a lot.

TRUE **FALSE**

232. Partner 1 likes reading.

233. Partner 2 sleeps a lot.

234. Partner 1 is more outgoing.

235. Partner 2 is addicted to social media.

236. Partner 1 loves luxurious life.

237. Partner 2 spends more time with their family.

238. Partner 1 is a bigger drama queen.

239. Partner 2 is always down to watch Netflix.

240. Partner 1 is a good dancer.

TRUE **FALSE**

241. Partner 2 knows how to cook.

242. Partner 1 sings a lot in the shower.

243. Partner 2 loves gym.

244. Partner 1 cheated on their ex.

245. Partner 2 worries too much about little things.

246. Partner 1 said "I love you" first.

247. Partner 2 is too gullible.

248. Partner 1 earns more.

249. Partner 2 is secure about finances.

250. Partner 1 was a good student.

Partner 1
Answers

Easy questions about everyday life

1.....................................

2.....................................

3.....................................

4.....................................

5.....................................

6.....................................

7.....................................

8.....................................

9.....................................

10....................................

11....................................

12....................................

13....................................

14....................................

15....................................

16....................................

17....................................

18....................................

19....................................

20....................................

21....................................

22....................................

23....................................

24....................................

25....................................

26....................................

27....................................

28....................................

29....................................

30....................................

In total: ....

Throwback to when we met

31.. 44..

32.. 45..

33.. 46..

34.. 47..

35.. 48..

36.. 49..

37.. 50..

38.. 51..

39.. 52..

40.. 53..

41.. 54..

42..

In total: ....

Food Checkup

55...

56...

57...

58...

59...

60...

61...

62...

63...

64...

65...

66...

67...

68...

69...

70...

71...

72...

73...

74...

75...

76...

77...

78...

79...

In total: ....

This or That

80. ....
81. ....
82. ....
83. ....
84. ....
85. ....
86. ....
87. ....
88. ....
89. ....
90. ....
91. ....
92. ....
93. ....
94. ....

95. ....
96. ....
97. ....
98. ....
99. ....
100. ....
101. ....
102. ....
103. ....
104. ....
105. ....
106. ....
107. ....
108. ....
109. ....

In total: ....

This or That

110...   115...

111...   116...

112...   117...

113...   118...

114...   119...

In total: ....

Who Is Most Likely To

120. ....

121. ....

122. ....

123. ....

124. ....

125. ....

126. ....

127. ....

128. ....

129. ....

130. ....

131. ....

132. ....

133. ....

134. ....

135. ....

136. ....

137. ....

138. ....

139. ....

140. ....

141. ....

142. ....

In total: ....

Future and Past

143................................... 151...................................

144................................... 152...................................

145................................... 153...................................

146................................... 154...................................

147................................... 155...................................

148................................... 156...................................

149................................... 157...................................

150...................................

In total: ....

What happens in bed, stays in bed

158. .... 168. ....

159. .... 169. ....

160. .... 170. ....

161. .... 171. ....

162. .... 172. ....

163. .... 173. ....

164. .... 174. ....

165. .... 175. ....

166. .... 176. ....

167. .... 177. ....

In total: ....

My favorite F words are Family and Friends

178..

179..

180..

181..

182..

183..

184..

185..

186..

187..

188..

189..

180..

191..

192..

193..

194..

195..

196..

197..

198..

In total: ....

Would your partner rather

199.. 212..

200.. 213..

202.. 214..

203.. 215..

204.. 216..

205.. 217..

206.. 218..

207.. 219..

208.. 220..

209.. 221..

210.. 222..

211..

In total: ....

True or False

223..
224..
225..
226..
227..
228..
229..
230..
231..
232..
233..
234..
235..
236..

237..
238..
238..
240..
241..
242..
243..
244..
245..
246..
247..
248..
249..
250..

In total: ....

Partner 2
Answers

Easy questions about everyday life

1. ....
2. ....
3. ....
4. ....
5. ....
6. ....
7. ....
8. ....
9. ....
10. ....
11. ....
12. ....
13. ....
14. ....
15. ....

16. ....
17. ....
18. ....
19. ....
20. ....
21. ....
22. ....
23. ....
24. ....
25. ....
26. ....
27. ....
28. ....
29. ....
30. ....

In total: ....

Throwback to when we met

31. ....
32. ....
33. ....
34. ....
35. ....
36. ....
37. ....
38. ....
39. ....
40. ....
41. ....
42. ....

44. ....
45. ....
46. ....
47. ....
48. ....
49. ....
50. ....
51. ....
52. ....
53. ....
54. ....

In total: ....

Food Checkup

55.. 68..
56.. 69..
57.. 70..
58.. 71..
59.. 72..
60.. 73..
61.. 74..
62.. 75..
63.. 76..
64.. 77..
65.. 78..
66.. 79..
67..

In total: ....

This or That

80..................................... 95.....................................
81..................................... 96.....................................
82..................................... 97.....................................
83..................................... 98.....................................
84..................................... 99.....................................
85..................................... 100...................................
86..................................... 101...................................
87..................................... 102...................................
88..................................... 103...................................
89..................................... 104...................................
90..................................... 105...................................
91..................................... 106...................................
92..................................... 107...................................
93..................................... 108...................................
94..................................... 109...................................

In total: ....

This or That

110.. 115..

111.. 116..

112.. 117..

113.. 118..

114.. 119..

In total: ....

Who Is Most Likely To

120. ....

121. ....

122. ....

123. ....

124. ....

125. ....

126. ....

127. ....

128. ....

129. ....

130. ....

131. ....

132. ....

133. ....

134. ....

135. ....

136. ....

137. ....

138. ....

139. ....

140. ....

141. ....

142. ....

In total: ....

Future and Past

143.................................... 151....................................

144.................................... 152....................................

145.................................... 153....................................

146.................................... 154....................................

147.................................... 155....................................

148.................................... 156....................................

149.................................... 157....................................

150....................................

In total: ....

What happens in bed, stays in bed

158.. 168..

159.. 169..

160.. 170..

161.. 171..

162.. 172..

163.. 173..

164.. 174..

165.. 175..

166.. 176..

167.. 177..

In total: ....

My favorite F words are Family and Friends

178... 189...

179... 180...

180... 191...

181... 192...

182... 193...

183... 194...

184... 195...

185... 196...

186... 197...

187... 198...

188...

In total: ....

Would your partner rather

199..

200..

202..

203..

204..

205..

206..

207..

208..

209..

210..

211..

212..

213..

214..

215..

216..

217..

218..

219..

220..

221..

222..

In total: ....

True or False

223..................................... 237.....................................

224..................................... 238.....................................

225..................................... 238.....................................

226..................................... 240.....................................

227..................................... 241.....................................

228..................................... 242.....................................

229..................................... 243.....................................

230..................................... 244.....................................

231..................................... 245.....................................

232..................................... 246.....................................

233..................................... 247.....................................

234..................................... 248.....................................

235..................................... 249.....................................

236..................................... 250.....................................

In total: ....

About the author

Natalie Styles - a young woman passionate about life, travels and relationships, born in late 90's. She is a flight attendant by profession, what she truly loves and what gives her a lot of joy. In her free time, Natalie cannot imagine a day without going to the gym. The main part of her life is self-development. Mostly, she spends time traveling and learning about relationships. She believes that the secret to a successful relationship is conversation. Recently, she has started a new adventure with Computer Graphics. She never gives up and always strives for excellence. *250 Quizzes For Couples: How Well Do You Really Know Me?* is her debut, but immediately after publishing this book, she started a new one.

Manufactured by Amazon.ca
Bolton, ON